MW01195669

The

DISCOVERY

of

WITCHES

A study of *Master Matthew Hopkins*
commonly call'd Witch Finder Generall

by The Rev.

MONTAGUE SUMMERS

together with a Reprint of
The Discovery of Witches
from the rare original of 1647

and

Collectanea:
WITCHCRAFT

Reprinted from Folk-Lore

BEING THE QUARTERLY TRANSACTIONS
OF THE FOLK-LORE SOCIETY.
JUNE 1939

by

G. B. GARDNER

I-H-O BOOKS

Frontispiece from the original edition of 1647

The Discovery of Witches

A Study of Master Matthew Hopkins

Sir Jeffery. Is there a Justice in *Lancashire* has so much skill in Witches as I have ? Nay, I'le speak a proud word, you shall turn me loose against any Witch-finder in *Europe*; I'd make an Ass of *Hopkins* if he were alive. Shadwell, *The Lancashire Witches,* I. (1681 ; 4to, 1682).

IN the earliest English codes of law, such as the statutes of Withraed, King of Kent, of Edward and Gunthrun, as well as those of Aethelstan and King Edgar, of Ethelred and Cnut ; in the most ancient Penitentials, as for example the famous collection of S. Theodore, seventh Archbishop of Canterbury, and the Confessional of Ecgberht, Archbishop of York, who received the pallium from Pope Gregory III in 735 ; in ecclesiastical canons and the decrees of secular witenagemot alike, there are laws, prohibitive and minatory, against sorcery and the practices of witchcraft, which were ever recognized as a very real and terrible evil. When S. Augustine, in the spring of 596, landed with his holy monks on the Isle of Thanet, he realized from the first moment that his battle would not only be against Pagan priests and their heathen hordes, but also against the dark unseen powers, who were not easily to be dislodged from the fair land of Britain. And in his contest, as in the contest of many another missionary from Rome, the labours of S. Boniface in Germany, of S. Francis Xavier in Malacca and Japan, and thousands more, he might literally have cried with S. Paul: "Our wrestling is not against flesh and blood, but against principalities and powers, against the rulers of the world of this darkness, against the spirits of wickedness in the high places." That the inhabitants of Britain already knew and dreaded the influences of these demon powers is shown by the fact that King Aethelberht at first suspected that this stranger from Italy, the southern land far over the seas, might be some mighty magician, and therefore he insisted that their first meeting should take place under a mighty oak, since here no baleful charm or horrid incantation could prevail. For the oak above all the forest is the sacred tree, throughout all lands and in all ages. The famous grove of Dodona, where Zeus was worshipped in the oracular oak, was the primeval sanctuary of Greece; and in primitive Italy every oak was sacred to Jupiter, the Latin counterpart of Zeus. The God of the oak, who spake in the roll and crash of thunder, was the supreme deity of the savage Aryans who dwelt in the heart of the virgin woods. Many scholars, indeed, believe that the word "Druids" means nothing more than "oak men," and, though the name was not derived from the Greek, they say that Pliny was substantially right when he connected Druid with δρῦς, and wrote: "Nihil habent Druidae (ita suos appellant magos) uisco, et arbore, in qua gignatur (si modo sit robur) sacratius. Iam per se roborum eligunt lucos, nec ulla sacra sine ea fronde conficiunt, ut inde appellati quoque interpretatione Graeca possint Druidae uideri." (*Hist. Nat.* XVI, 95.)

In the year 723 S. Boniface clove to the ground with his sharp axe at Geismar, near Fritzlar, a huge oak which went by the name of *Donares Eih*, "the oak of Donar," which the old chronicler translates as *robur Iouis*, since Donor or Thunar, who is the Norse Thor, is the equivalent of Jupiter. It has been said, and with truth, that the fall of this tree was the destruction of heathenism in Germany. Among the Slavs, the image at Novgorod of Perun, who is the counterpart of Zeus and Jupiter, was honoured by a huge pyre of oak logs which blazed before him day and night, and if by chance it were extinguished, his ministers expiated this negligence, which was considered the grossest profanity provoking the wrath of the god, by the instant sacrifice of their lives.

It is well, then, to remember that the first conference which the English King held with S. Augustine beneath the shade of the immemorial oaks of Kent was not arranged to take place there for any mere convenience sake, but with a very solemn and mysterious purpose, since the shadow of the trees was regarded as a spiritual safeguard and protection.

The earliest references to witchcraft among native historians are mostly concerned with superstitious rites and the clandestine, or it may be overt, observance of pagan festivals by obscene dances and lewd assemblies. William of Malmesbury tells the story of the Witch of Berkeley, and this is assigned to the year 852, although in its details

7

it might well have been a history of the sixteenth century. During the reign of King John, in 1209, a woman named Galiena was charged with sorcery, but acquitted after the ordeal of the hot iron. In 1233 Hubert, Earl of Kent, was accused " upon pretence that he stole out of the King's Jewel-house a stone that would make a man invisible; and gave it to *Lewellyn* the King's Enemy. Also that he had drawn the King's Favour to himself, above others, by Sorceries." In 1279 a man killed a woman commonly reputed to be a witch, who had upon some occasion visited his house and assaulted him. He was fined, but had already fled from justice.

In 1303 one of the chief peers of the realm, Walter Langton, Bishop of Coventry and Lichfield, was accused before Boniface VIII of witchcraft, and the Pope ordered a full inquiry into the charges, but the incriminated prelate was able completely to clear himself.[1]

On a charge of black magic, in 1371, a man was arrested at Southwark and brought before Sir John Knivet of the King's Bench. He was discovered in most incriminating circumstances, since he had upon a him a skull, the head of a corpse, and a book of goety. There can be no reasonable doubt that he had been reciting a demoniacal invocation, but the court merely made him swear that he would never perform any occult rite or rehearse runes and cantrips of any kind whatsoever, whereupon apparently without any further penalty he was released from prison, the talismanic

---

[1] " Erat episcopus in regno Angliæ et alibi publice defamatus quod diabolo homagium fecerat, et eum fuerat osculatus in tergo eique locutus multotiens."

skull, the head, and the black breviary being confiscated and publicly burned in Tothill Fields.

It will be noted that these examples are few and far between, and when the offenders are brought to justice they seem to be dealt with very lightly, nor, so far as we can judge, did they make much noise at the time. There were, however, a number of other cases of particular gravity which caused resounding scandal throughout the realm. Yet their heinous guilt may be considered accidental, and to consist not so much in the actual practice of witchcraft, as in the damning fact that witchcraft was mingled with politics, generally with high treason and a direct attempt upon the life of the Sovereign. Thus in 1324 no less than twenty-seven defendants were tried at Coventry for having employed and richly feed two necromancers to undertake the slaying of King Edward; of the royal favourites, the Le Despensers, together with a number of other prominent and noble supporters of the royal cause. In 1441 the Duchess of Gloucester was charged with having consulted spirits as to the probable duration of the King's life, and with having employed certain witches speedily to bring about the death of Henry VI so that the throne might be vacant for her husband. In these dark businesses she had the assistance of a whole coven of witches, the chief of whom, Roger Bolingbroke, a notorious necromancer, was actually entertained in the Duke's household. The principal compt against the Duchess was that of high treason, and Bolingbroke was accused of "werchyrye of sorcery against the King." He was found guilty in the highest degree; hanged at Tyburn, beheaded, and quartered, his head being exposed upon London Bridge, and the limbs over the gates of Hereford, Oxford, Cambridge, and York. The Duchess herself was condemned by the ecclesiastical courts, presided over by the Bishops of London, Lincoln, and Norwich, who sentenced her to do public penance through the streets of London on three several days, a Monday, a Wednesday, and a Friday. She was then imprisoned for life at Chester, whence she was afterwards removed for greater seclusion to Peel Castle in the Isle of Man. Upon the night of Bolingbroke's arrest she had fled for sanctuary to Westminster Abbey, but was refused admission by the Abbot on the ground of spiritual offence. This is a very curious circumstance, and it seems altogether uncertain whether such right of sanctuary could canonically be disallowed. In fact it is fairly plain that, without some particular and direct injunction from the Holy See, sanctuary should not be withheld. However, it must be remembered that the Abbot of Westminster was a highly important personage with a seat in the House of Lords. The Abbey was in close proximity to the Royal Palace, and it seems probable that political motives influenced the unusual decision in this especial instance.

The feature that is rendered most prominent by so famous a case, as well as by the majority of the earlier trials for witchcraft—that is to say, until the middle of the sixteenth century—is that the penalties for sorcery alone do not seem to have been notoriously severe, and, save in the rarest exceptions, this offence was only punished by death when there were aggravating circumstances, and almost invariably the additional charge was that of high treason. This is very clearly shown owing to the fact that when the Duchess of

Gloucester and those whom she had employed were condemned, a witch named Margery Jourdemain, originally from Eye in Suffolk, who was implicated, suffered at the stake in Smithfield on October 27th, 1441. Nine years before, this same woman had been prosecuted for practising black magic. On May 9th, 1432, the Constable of Windsor brought before the Privy Council three persons suspected "pro sorcerye," since their offences had fallen within his commission. The accused were John Virley, a cleric ; John Ashwell, a mendicant friar ; and Margery Jourdemain, who was presented as a married woman. Although the charges were proven, so little heed was paid to the matter that the two men were released upon giving security, and the witch was without difficulty bailed by her husband. The proceedings then terminated, and the whole matter completely dropped. This leniency may be noted with some surprise, and we should particularly remark the very different measures that were taken when any suspicion of conspiracy, by spells and charms or otherwise, touching the life of the King, was aroused. There is yet another point which it may not be impertinent to mention here. Margery Jourdemain was, as we have seen, burned in Smithfield, and it is almost invariably stated, even by writers of weight and authority, that burning was in England the judicial punishment for the crime of witchcraft. Although I have traversed this mistake more than once, the error is so obstinate and persists so widely that it will assuredly not be labour lost to contradict it once again. That the stake was always the punishment for witches has not merely been affirmed but most resolutely maintained. For example, treating of *The*

Witchcraft and Vagrancy Acts, E. P. Hewitt, Esq., K.C., in a very valuable paper[1] says : " Sir Matthew Hale in 1664 had before him at Bury St. Edmunds two women charged with witchcraft—they were convicted and burned. And a few years later, eighteen persons were burned at S. Osyth, in Essex, for the same offence." This is incorrect, and contemporary records might be cited in both instances to show that these persons were hanged. For convenience sake I will only refer to Bishop Francis Hutchinson's *Historical Essay Concerning Witchcraft*,[2] where he notes (p. 54) under the year 1664 : " *Amy Duny* and *Rose Cullender*, try'd before the Lord Chief Baron *Hale*, at *Bury St. Edmunds*, in *Suffolk*, and were hanged, maintaining their Innocence." In chapter viii he gives a very detailed account of this case.

The prosecutions at S. Osyth were not " a few years later " but eighty-two years before, in 1582, and although it is doubtful how many persons were executed, it is certain that they were hanged.[3]

Miss M. A. Murray, *The Witch-Cult in Western Europe*,[4] writes in an off-hand way : " The belief that the witch must be burned and the ashes scattered was so engraved in the popular mind that, when the severity of the laws began to relax, remonstrances were made by or to the authorities."

[1] *The Solicitor's Journal*, June 25th, 1927, pp. 503-4.
[2] The Second Edition, 1720.
[3] It is generally believed that twelve or thirteen suffered, but Reginald Scot raises the number to seventeen or eighteen. It may be noted that Mr. Hewitt concludes his article by saying : " In 1895 one Bridget Cleary was burned as a witch in County Tipperary." Surely so unqualified a statement is very misleading. The terrible Ballyvadhen tragedy was that of a poor woman who was placed on the kitchen fire by her own family and burned to death, not on account of any supposed witchcraft, but in the belief that the real wife had been stolen and that she was a changeling substituted by the fairies, who when their clurichaune was subjected to the ordeal of fire would snatch it away and restore the stolen wife safe and sound.
[4] P. 161.

She then quotes a record of the Scotch General Assembly of 1649, which has nothing at all to do with the matter under consideration; and this is followed up by a remark passed when certain witches were hanged at Maidstone in 1652 to the effect that such offenders ought to be burned, which is nothing more than an impertinent expression of the continental opinion. The third case next adduced, that of Ann Foster, who was hanged at Northampton in 1674, is very arguable, since, although the charge of witchcraft was certainly brought, the fact upon which she was condemned was that she had not only maimed and killed above thirty sheep belonging to her neighbour, a well-to-do farmer, but had also set on fire several of his barns and even his house. Miss Murray has attempted too sweeping a generalization, which so far as England was concerned is inaccurate.[1] In Scotland and upon the continent the punishment of witchcraft was almost universally the stake, but in England it was the gallows tree. It is, of course, wholly irrelevant to quote Scottish or French trials as bearing upon English practice, but this is continually done, and the idea that witches were burned (even in England) has so impressed itself upon the popular imagination that it will be a matter of extreme difficulty to gain acceptance for the correct view. Indeed it is a question whether it be worth while to press the point, that is for popular instruction. The stake is much more horrible, much more mediæval and picturesque than hanging, and so let romanticist and story-book burn their

[1] The theory (*The Witch-Cult in Western Europe*, p. 161) that the burning of a witch was " the sacrifice of the incarnate deity . . . consummated at the hands of the public executioner" is so fantastic and entirely preposterous as to elude all serious consideration.

witches if they will. But surely the scholar and historian, the professed students of the subject, these at any rate should not follow the ignorant to do ill, seemingly because they are loath to be at the labour of controverting a popular and fast-grounded, if erroneous, opinion.

Yet in order to justify themselves they will quote the case of Jane Lakeland who in 1645 was burned at Ipswich, as they say, for sorcery. However, there is more in this particular example than readily appears. Jane Lakeland was charged with witchcraft, and she would, since the accusation was proven, doubtless have been hanged. The particular malice of her guilt lay in another direction. She had killed her husband, by her charms, it was averred. Now for a woman to commit either high treason (any attempt, direct or indirect, upon the life of the sovran) or petty treason (the murder of a husband by a wife, the murder of a master or mistress by a servant) was punished with the penalty of death at the stake.[1] It was indifferent whether Jane Lakeland had killed her husband by an evil spell or by poison or by steel; the crime constituted petty treason, and accordingly she was burned. So in the same way, in the reign of Henry VI, Margery Jourdemain was burned at Smithfield for high treason, which, as it happened, was in this instance complicated with sorcery. On a charge of sorcery alone, as we have seen, she had some years before easily escaped punishment. It may be remarked that Bishop Hutchinson notes: "About this time *Jane Lakeland* was either hanged or burned at *Ipswich*." Evidently there was some

[1] This penalty remained in force until June 5th, 1790, when by 30 George III, c. 48 (1790), it was provided that women under this sentence should be hanged. For an account of the whole question see my *Geography of Witchcraft*, pp. 155-7.

14

doubt with regard to this execution, for Hutchinson spared no pains to arrive at facts. So far as possible, he made a personal investigation and instituted searching inquiries concerning all cases of witchcraft that had come under the knowledge of any persons then living. His interest in these matters had been awakened as early as 1700, and since when he was writing his book he was Vicar of St. James's at Bury St. Edmunds, it is not at all improbable that he had spoken with those whose fathers or relatives had often described to them the famous trial and execution which took place at Ipswich, not so very many miles away, some five and fifty years before.

From the reign of Henry VI to that of Henry VIII many important cases might be brought forward in which charges of sorcery were essentially conjoined with charges of high treason. For example, in 1483 " King *Richard*, being of the House of *York*, attainted for sorcery several that supported the Line of *Lancaster*. As the Countess of *Richmond*, Mother of *Henry* the 7th; Dr. *Morton*, afterwards Archbishop of *Canterbury* ; Dr. *Lewis*, *William Knevit*, and *Thomas Nandyck* of *Cambridge*, called Conjurer : *Nandyck* was taken, and condemned, but saved by the Parliament." Common gossip even whispered that the influence of Cardinal Wolsey over Henry VIII was due to magic ; and it is well known that as soon as this tyrant King had grown tired of Anne Bullen he was at pains to spread the report that he had " made this marriage seduced by witchcraft." When the Duke of Buckingham was condemned, in 1521, on a charge of high treason, one of the gravest accusations deposed that he had consulted a monk of the Charter House at Hinton in Somerset to inquire by cristallomantia whether the King had many more days. In 1541 Lord Hungerford was beheaded "for procuring certain persons to conspire that they might know how long the King's Grace should live," and in the same year an act was passed against all who "have used and occupied wichecrafts, inchauntmentes, and sorceries to the distruccion of their neighbours persones and goodes." Archbishop Cranmer, too, in his Articles of Visitation, 1549, has the following : "Item, you shall inquire, whether you know any that use charms, sorcery, enchantments, witchcraft, southsaying, or any like crafts, invented by the Devil."

Although, of course, there had been in former years one or two special cases, it may fairly be said that it was not until the reign of Queen Elizabeth that the prosecution of witches became general in England, and that witchcraft in itself was regarded as a capital offence. Very soon after the accession of the new Queen a Bill directed against witchcraft was drafted, and in 1563 this measure passed on to the statute-book and became English law. The earlier accusations had for the most part been brought against persons of condition and quality ; and, as we have remarked, some political bias was generally to be suspected. But now humbler game was started, and the crusade was directed in full fury against those who were old and obscure, who were owl-blasted, indigent, and wretched. In a letter dated November 2nd, 1559, John Jewel, who had been conducting a visitation of the western counties, writes : " The number of witches and sorceresses had everywhere become enormous." Trials and executions soon began to succeed

16

each other with breathless rapidity, and the pamphlet literature of the time is so very considerable that even the briefest bibliography must fill many pages. It is possible only to mention a very few of the more important trials. In 1566 Mother Waterhouse and Alice Chandler were hanged at Chelmsford; thirteen years later three more women were executed in the same town; in 1579 four were hanged at Abingdon; and in 1582 occurred the notorious case of the witches of S. Osyth, a hamlet to the north-east of Chelmsford. In the following year Mother Gabley was hanged at King's Lynn. In 1589 there was a fresh alarm at Chelmsford, when three notorious witches went to the gallows. In 1593 took place the famous prosecutions at Warboys in Huntingdonshire, when the whole Samuel family, father, mother, and daughter, were hanged for having killed Lady Cromwell by a charm and cast malefic spells upon the house of Throckmorton. Sir Samuel Cromwell bequeathed a sum of £40 annually to Queen's College, Cambridge, in order that on each Lady Day a divine of the college should deliver a sermon from the pulpit at Huntingdon, and this solemn discourse was to have Witchcraft as the theme. The sermon was still preached during the early years of the nineteenth century, but I am unable to say whether the practice is still in force; and even if, as it would appear, it was for some time discontinued, in these days it might be renewed with notable profit both to men's intellects and to the health of their souls. In 1595 two witches were executed at Barnet and one at Brainford; in 1596 Mother Cooke was hanged at Leicester; in 1598 Elizabeth Housegoe was executed at King's Lynn; in 1599 Oliffe

Bartham was hanged at Bury St. Edmunds. Just a few names have been mentioned here and there at random; it were superfluous to give year after year in the various counties of England the long tale of executions for sorcery and black magic. It is plain that England swarmed with persons who were practising the most dangerous crafts, and we must remember that probably not a tithe of the guilty were discovered and brought to open justice.

From the earliest days there had been in Scotland prosecutions for witchcraft, and here the penalty was usually the stake, whether the crime involved high treason or whether there was no suspicion at all of any political intrigue. Thus among the laws attributed to Kenneth I (d. 860), and which even if this be not their exact original are doubtless very early, is one statute which directs that all witches and persons who invoke spirits " and use to seek upon them helpe, let them be burned to death." These penalties remained permanently in force, although from time to time they were strengthened and renewed. Thus when, in 1563, the ninth parliament of Queen Mary passed an Act making all matters of witchcraft a capital offence there immediately followed a regular crusade against the guilty and the suspect. In 1590, under James VI, occurred one of the most famous episodes in the whole history of witchcraft, the prosecution of the North Berwick covens, when there had met at the old haunted church of North Berwick upon All Hallows E'en warlocks and Satanists to the number of at least one hundred and fifty—other and reliable accounts say nearly double that tale—who, it is now clearly established, were organized by the Earl of Bothwell, to assist him in his aiming at the throne. Seventy persons of those implicated were put upon their trial, and the King himself took an active part in the judicial proceedings. The whole case is extremely important from every point of view, since persons of quality were involved as well as losels of the meanest condition. We here also have evidence that witchcraft was a world-wide conspiracy, an integral part of that huge revolutionary movement which anarchy is always fostering, and which throughout history has continually broken forth in subversive movements and dark plots against civilization.

Archbishop Spotswood, Primate of S. Andrews,[1] writing of the year 1591, says that " most of this Winter was spent in Examination of Witches and Sorcerers. *Bothwel* the Conspirator had consulted with *Agnes Symson.*"[2] In 1597, at Edinburgh, King James published his famous *Daemonologie, in Forme of a Dialogue, Diuided into three Bookes*, a work which, when he succeeded to the English throne half a dozen years later, was naturally accepted as authoritative in England as it had already been received in his northern kingdom. No doubt many of the records are either missing, or have not yet been closely examined, but it is remarkable that the numbers of persons condemned to death in England under James I are by no means so many as were popularly supposed. There are indeed actually not more than fifty instances during a reign of two-and-twenty years, and these include the notorious prosecution of the Lancashire Witches in 1612. There were, of course, a great many more trials, and the offenders received various sentences, some

[1] He was translated to the metropolitan see on the death of Archbishop Gladstanes in 1615.
[2] Rather Agnes Sampson, an " elder witch."

light and some severe, but the fact remains that less than half a hundred persons suffered on the gallows for this offence, and it must be remembered that in those days hanging was the penalty for delinquencies which to-day would be considered sufficiently to be met with a petty fine or even a magisterial caution.

It is yet more remarkable that during the reign of Charles I, that is to say whilst the King was in full enjoyment of his royal prerogative, which may fairly be said to have been first seriously hampered at the outbreak of the Great Rebellion in 1642, there were until this date but seven recorded executions for witchcraft, and of these two rest upon very doubtful evidence. In the case of the second Lancashire prosecutions, 1633-34, when seventeen persons were tried and condemned, the King reprieved all who lay under sentence and they were shortly released from prison. The immediate change which took place in 1642 and the Parliamentary prosecutions which raged far and wide during the next eighteen years are certainly amazing. Without going so far as entirely to accept the figures of Dr. Zachary Grey, who in his notes upon *Hudidras* says that under the Long Parliament " betwixt three and four thousands " were hanged, we are bound most certainly to affirm that whilst Cromwell had the upper hand the number of executions was far greater in England than ever before or ever since.[1]

[1] *Hudibras*, II, Canto iii, 143-4, Dr. Grey's note is : " Dr. Meric Casaubon in his Preface to Dr. *Dee's Book of Spirits* observes : That nine hundred Men and Women suffer'd in *Lorain* for Witchcraft in the Compass of a few Years : And *Ludovicus Paramo*, that the Inquisition, within the space of one hundred and fifty years, has burnt thirty thousand Witches. *Baker's History of the Inquisition*, p. 186. But our enthusiasts much exceeded both. Mr. *Ady* says that in *Scotland* some thousands were burnt in those Times. (Dr. Hutchinson, p. 38.) I have somewhere seen an Account of betwixt three and four thousands, that suffer'd in the King's Dominions from the

Moreover it cannot escape notice that the prosecutions were particularly rife in those counties which were notoriously disloyal to the King and fell entirely under Puritan influence.

It was at this juncture that there came into prominence the most notorious figure in the annals of English witchcraft, a man who was wholly worthy to be the accredited emissary of the Parliament in these dark and difficult businesses. We may here not impertinently quote Richard Baxter's summary of the affair which he gave in the last of his many works to be published during his long life, *The Certainty of the Worlds of Spirits, fully evinced, by unquestionable histories of Apparitions and Witch-crafts, Operations, Voices, etc. ; . . . Written for the Conviction of Sadducees and Infidels,* 8vo, London, 1691.[1] This runs as follows : " The hanging of a great Number of witches in *Suffolk* and *Essex*, by the Discovery of one *Hopkins* in 1645 and 1646, is famously known. Mr. *Calamy* went along with the Judges in the Circuit, to hear their Confessions, and see that there were no Fraud or Wrong done them. I spake with many understanding, pious and credible Persons, that lived in the Countries, and some that went to them to the Prisons. Among the rest, an old *Reading* Parson named *Lowis*, not far from *Framlingham*, was one that was hanged ; who confessed that he had two imps, that one of them was always

Year 1640 to the King's Restoration." *Hudibras* . . . with Large Annotations . . . by Zachary Grey, LL.D., London, 1744, Vol. II, p. 11. The *De origine et progressu officii Sanctae Inquisitionis* of Ludovico à Paramo was published at Madrid, 1598. Hutchinson in his *Historical Essay Concerning Witchcraft*, Second Edition, London, 1720, p. 51, *sub anno* 1649, has : " Great Numbers burnt in *Scotland* in those unsettled Times. Mr. *Ady* saith many thousands." *A Candle in the Dark* by Thomas Ady was printed London, 1656.

[1] *Term Catalogues*, Michaelmas (November). Baxter died December 8th, 1691.

putting him on doing Mischief, and (he being near the Sea) as he saw a Ship under Sail, it moved him to send him to sink the Ship, and he consented, and saw the Ship sink before him. One penitent Woman confessed, that her Mother lying sick, and she looking to her, somewhat like a Mole ran into the Bed to her, which she being startled at, her Mother bad her not fear it, but gave it her, saying, Keep this in a Pot by the fire, &c. and thou shalt never want. She did as she was bid ; shortly after a poor Boy (seemingly) came in, and ask'd leave to sit and warm him at the Fire, and when he was gone, she found Money under the stool ; and afterwards oft did so again, and at last laid hold of her, and drew Blood of her, and she made no other Compact with the Devil, but that her Imps sucked her Blood ; and as I heard she was delivered. Abundance of sad Confessions were made by them ; by which some testified, that there are certain Punishments which they were to undergo, if they did not some hurt as was appointed them."

Matthew Hopkins was the son of James Hopkins, minister of Wenham, Suffolk. Of his youth little is known, but it is evident from his pamphlet that he was able to pen a matter pretty cleverly and concisely, and his special pleading is forcible and fluent enough. It is obvious that he must have been an orthodox Puritan of the conventionally popular opiniatry, which, as his party had gained the ascendancy, proved of the narrowest and most intolerant kind. This may be sufficiently gathered from the records of his activities, nor would the Parliament have entrusted these affairs to a man of another sort. His colleague, John Stearne, was a furious Calvinist, and it is evident that they must have shared the same ideas, which were regarded with highest approval by Dr. Edmund Calamy, a divine who distinguished himself by his violent diatribes against King Charles I, and who when, at the Restoration, he was invited to preach before the King, caused a good deal of scandal by refusing to wear a surplice, and shortly, flouting all attempts at reconciliation, exhibited himself so obstinate an agitator that Dr. Sheldon, Bishop of London, was obliged forcibly to restrain his heterodoxy. That an extremist of this school should have fostered the crusade of Hopkins very clearly demonstrates the bitter creed of those concerned. There is one important point which must not here be passed over, and the full significance of which will be very apparent, to wit although Matthew Hopkins was undoubtedly a man of no small energy and of considerable force of character, possessing indeed a personality to be reckoned with, as his career clearly shows, yet his religious proclivities are nowhere protruded or even emphasized in circumstances which might well have been thought to have been most favourable to the exhibition of an unusual pietism and sanctimoniousness, which it is quite certain his fellow enthusiastists of the same kidney would have deployed and exaggerated on every possible occasion. It seems strange that it is possible to find a good word to say of Matthew Hopkins, but it is only fair to notice that although he was a humbug, he was not at any rate a canting humbug. The explanation of this probably lies in the fact that he was too soulless even to make a pretence of religious zeal when such hypocrisy would not any better play his game nor put another penny in his pocket. His position was that of the layman and the lawyer, a standpoint that served his purpose admirably well. At the same time it cannot escape remark that in a period of the wildest fanaticism his utterances from a Puritan point of view are singularly lukewarm and lacking in that violence of rant which was so much emulated and admired.

It seems probable that Hopkins[1] at first found the legal profession singularly unremunerative, or else he had no opportunity of displaying his particular skill, since he is spoken of as "a lawyer of but little note" at Ipswich, whence with the idea, no doubt, of bettering his prospects he removed to the small town of Manningtree[2] in Essex. It was here, as he has himself told us, that an accident diverted his attention in another direction and that he saw a fine career awaiting the man who, taking advantage of the terrible disorders of the time, could employ for his own benefit the malevolence and rancour which are invariably most dangerous when bloodshed and anarchy threaten the stability of religion and society in some unfortunate land.

It does not seem probable that Hopkins had made any great preparations when he so rashly and so wrongfully embarked upon a concern which should only be undertaken under the stern pressure of actual duty. It is a business from which many men, and these not the least brave, have shrunk, inasmuch as all those whose terrible duty it is to investigate these matters, whether as in the past in the Episcopal or Inquisitorial Courts, or whether in judicial and scholarly

[1] Obviously he must not be identified with the Matthew Hopkins of Southwark who in 1644 complained that he was unable to pay the crushing taxes. See *Calendar of the Proceedings of the Committee for Advance of Money*, 1642-56, I, 457.
[2] At the present time (1928) the population of Manningtree is 870.

volumes, are aware that they lay themselves open to aspersion and ignorant obloquy, to detraction and even personal abuse, which they must expect and patiently endure. It is, then, certainly not an easy, and by no means an enviable task to treat of these difficult businesses. The precipitancy, one might almost say the impetuosity, with which Matthew Hopkins rushed in, do not in truth augur that gravity and sincerity, that probity and impartial spirit, which are so necessary for any practical inquiry into occult matters. It would appear that from the first he enjoyed notoriety, and even more surely that along these lines he saw a chance of reaping those rich emoluments which seemed to be denied him by the obscure and humdrum routine of the legal avocation in the smallest of country towns.

With the works of the great demonologists it is tolerably plain that he had no acquaintance, and since such a course of study is the very first requisite for one who proposes to deal with these esoterica, either, as was then possible, in the court of law, or even merely from a historical and—if you will—a literary point of view, it is obvious that he was heavily handicapped when he began his course. We are certainly correct in saying that even the supreme authority of the *Malleus Maleficarum* was unknown to him ; that he had not read Bodin, Grilland, Godelman, Boguet, Remy, Guazzo, and the rest. There is no indication that he was a scholar, and the works of these writers being technical to a degree demand not merely an erudite Latinity but also an especial intensive technical training. Hopkins was familiar with the *Daemonologie* of King James, who reproduces something of the older authors although at second hand. He seems to have known Richard Bernard's[1] *Guide to Grand Jurymen*, 1627, a book with which he would no doubt have become familiar during his professional training. This author had made a special study of the legal aspect of witchcraft, and he resumes many of the arguments of both continental and native writers. He is conscious that terrible mistakes have been made costing human lives, and he believes that much supposed witchcraft is due to the extraordinary self-deception of the feeble-minded, who are often crazy for notoriety at any cost and by any means. He freely allows that there have been grave errors of justice owing to credulity and inexperience. He concludes that rumours of magic are often " the vain conceits of the addle-headed, or of silly fooles or of pratling gossips or of superstitiously fearful ; or of fansieful melancholicks, or of discomposed and crased wits." Nevertheless he is thoroughly convinced that, in spite of much hysteria, many impostures, and a good deal of ignorance, witchcraft is a very real and true thing, and when actually detected and proven it should be dealt with most rigorously according to law. In this he somewhat resembles John Cotta, the Northampton physician, who, in his *The Triall of Witchcraft*, 1616, puts forward what might be called the medical side of the case from a rationalizing point of view, namely that witchcraft is a stern fact, but that it is rare, and that the vast majority of instances can but prove the result of mental disorders and hallucinations. Yet he was bound to allow that the testimony of sober and reliable witnesses or the plain discovery of occult practices must be considered sufficient to condemn a witch.

[1] 1568-1641. Bernard was Vicar of Batcombe, Somerset.

Another book with which Matthew Hopkins was almost certainly well acquainted was *The Wonderfull Discoverie of Witches in the countie of Lancaster. With the Arraignment and Triall of Nineteene notorious Witches, at the Assizes and Gaole deliverie, holden at the Castle of Lancaster, upon Munday, the seventeenth of August last,* 1612. *Before Sir James Altham, and Sir Edward Bromley.* London, 1613. This was the work of Thomas Potts, a lawyer, who was very active in the affair.

There can be no doubt at all that Hopkins himself was a firm believer in witchcraft, and the particular infamy which has branded his name with more than ordinary turpitude does not lie in the fact that he prosecuted so large a number of trials and was so eager in his quest, but in the baseness and unscrupulousness of his motives, which made him no better than a common murderer, inasmuch as to fill his purse, to achieve power and a name, he used a black and damning crime, the guilt of which in those feverish days of terror and civil strife it was perilously easy to affix and peculiarly difficult to disprove. Men have always been apt and are still ready to charge their opponents, whether theological or political, with the vilest vices and the most unspeakable enormities. Probably this is because subconsciously they believe that an individual who can sin so grossly in one instance, the most vital point, must be guilty of the whole catalogue of crime, since the greater includes the less. Matthew Hopkins was not moved by any considerations such as this, which, however unfortunate, can at least be comprehended and understood. How far he was sincere in his first prosecution of the coven who met hard by his house at Manningtree may remain an open question, but it is fairly evident that having once tasted blood, having won a fearful respect and well lined his pockets, he determined to ply his new trade for all that it was worth in every direction. It must be acknowledged that everything was ready to his hand. In March, 1644, as he himself tells us, he made his first discovery. There seems no reason to dispute the fact that he did by chance light upon a company of witches, and although the confessions were embroidered with many extravagant and impossible details the charges of sorcery brought against these women were probably correct in the main. It is stated that the members of the local witch society assembled on a Friday night, and although it is true that in different countries and at different times the day of the week considerably varies, there is none the less a preponderance of evidence which points to Friday as being most generally favoured. De Lancre says that in the Basses-Pyrénées the assemblies took place " on three particular nights, Monday, Wednesday, and Friday."[1] The famous and learned Henry Boguet in his *Discours des Sorciers*, Lyons, 1603, c. xix, *Du iour du Sabbat*, writes as follows : " I'ay estimé autrefois que le Sabbat se tenoit seulement la nuict du ieudy, d'autāt que tous les Sorciers que i'ay veu, l'ont ainsi r'apporté : mais depuis que i'ay leu que quelques vns de la mesme secte ont confessé, qu'ils s'assembloyēt, les vns la nuict d'entre le lundy & le mardy, les autres la nuict d'entre le Vendredy & le Samedy, les autres la nuict qui precedoit le Ieudy, ou le Dimenche, de là i'ay conclu qu'il n'y auoit point de iour

[1] " Les Sorciers le vont adorer trois nuicts durant, celle du Lundy, du Mercredy, & du Vendredy." *Tableau de l'inconstance des mauvais anges.* Paris, 1612, p. 62.

prefix pour le Sabbat, & que les Sorciers y vōt lors qu'ils y sont mādéz par Satā.

"I'adiousteray icy ce qu' Antide Colas à cōfessé à ce propos, sçauoir que par enuiron sept ans elle auoit esté au Sabbat à vn chacun bon iour de l'année, comme à Noel, à Pasques, à la feste Dieu, & autres iours semblables, & que pour la derniere fois elle y fut vn soir des festes de Pasques en la Combe Sainete Marie, ou se retrouuerent enuiron quarante personnes : & disoit de plus, que le soir de Noel precedent, elle y fut entre la messe de la minuict & celle du point du iour : voila comme aux bons iours ce malin celebre ses assemblées, & retire la creature du service de Dieu." At the trial of Louis Gaufridi, Maria de Sains, a witness who was examined on May 17th-19th, 1614, asserted that Wednesday and Friday were the two nights especially chosen for the sabbats of blasphemy and the Satanic eucharist, and Hopkins records that on Friday the Essex witches met close to his house and "had their severall solemne sacrifices there offered to the Devill." Upon the information of Hopkins the following persons were taken into custody, Elizabeth Clarke, Ann West and her daughter Rebecca, Ann Leach, Helen Clarke, and Elizabeth Gooding. The local Justices of the Peace, men of the most inflamed fanaticism, Sir Harbottle Grimston and Sir Thomas Bowes, were not slow to listen to the charges, and Hopkins himself has detailed the tortures by which the wretched creatures whom he had accused were brought to confess. Another worthy now appears upon the scenes in the shape of John Stearne, who was to show himself a most energetic colleague and coadjutor. Ann

West, who had "been suspected as a witch many yeers since, and suffered imprisonment for the same," made most ample confession, and indeed before long nearly thirty persons were involved. Immediately there was abundance of local evidence. Richard Edwards had lost many of his cattle owing to a mysterious distemper, and even worse, his child had fallen sick, "rowling the eyes," and died. He swore that it had been destroyed by Ann Leech and Elizabeth Gooding. The latter was also accused by one Robert Taylor of having lamed and then killed his horse. Prudence Hart had been seized with extraordinary pains, and " she believed Rebecca West and Ann West the cause of her pains." So the tale went on, ever gathering fresh details and fresh accusations.

One of the most extraordinary features of these cases was the endless information which was supplied by all parties, accusers and accused alike, concerning the witches' familiars or attendant imps. Since Hopkins has given himself fullest details concerning this point in his pamphlet, it is hardly necessary to enlarge upon it at any great length, and in fact to do so would entail writing a lengthy monograph treating of this one subject alone. We may say that Rebecca West swore that when she was at the house of Elizabeth Clarke, where she had been conducted by her mother, who "told the said Rebecca, shee must keepe secret what soever shee saw, wither they were then going; and the said Rebecca promised so to doe " ; they found already assembled Ann Leach, Elizabeth Gooding, Helen Clarke, and the house-keeper Elizabeth Clarke, " and that forthwith the Devill appeared to them in the shape of a dogge ; afterwards in the shape of two kitlyns ; then in the shape of two dogges ; and that the said familiars did doe homage in the first place to the said Elizabeth Clarke, and skipped up into her lap and kissed her ; and then went and kissed all that were in the roome, except the said Rebecca." But when Rebecca had been sworn a witch, "the Devill came into her lap, and kissed her, and promised to doe for her what she could desire." Ann Cooper, the wife of John Cooper of Clacton, confessed that she " had three black impes called by the names of Wynowe, Jeso, and Panu." Margaret Moone confessed to Henry Cornwall that she had " twelve imps, and called them by their names ; of which he remembers onely these following : Jesus,[1] Jockey, Sandy, Mrit, Elizabeth, and Collyn." Marian Hocket had three imps, and " the said Marian called them by the names of Littleman, Pretty-Man, and Dainty." Exactly similar circumstances are recorded of all the accused. A curious detail is that no less than eight persons testified that they had on various occasions seen one or another of these imps in antic shapes or forms, and their several accounts substantially agree. The question arises how is this to be explained ? It is, of course, easy enough to say that it was all a delusion. If we argue upon these lines it will not be difficult to come to the conclusion that no human evidence is worth anything at all. We may accept just what fits in with our own prejudices and our own theory, and anything that is difficult of explanation may be dismissed as an error or a mistake. The spectators

[1] This is not possible. It is further alleged that the witch when summoning her familiars cried : " Come Christ, come Christ, come Mounsier, come Mounsier." But there is some confusion. To name the Sanctissimum Nomen would be to banish the familiars and dissolve the enchantment.

must have seen something to account for these phenomena.

The trials took place at Chelmsford on July 29th, 1645, Robert Rich, Earl of Warwick, being President of the Court. Hopkins says that twenty-nine were condemned, and Stearne records about twenty-eight. It is certain that four were hanged at Manningtree, and ten at Chelmsford, the rest probably being executed in other towns or villages throughout the district. Hopkins had now covered himself with great glory and presently he extended his operations into Suffolk, since the confessions of Elizabeth Clarke had implicated a number of persons living in that county, and it is hardly too much to say that a terrible panic incontinently began to spread throughout the whole of East Anglia. Hopkins was accompanied in his dreaded visitations by his jackal John Stearne, and by a female assistant one Goody Phillips. Hutchinson writes : " You must know then, that in the Years 1644, 1645, and 1646, *Matthew Hopkins*, of *Manningtree* in *Essex*, and one *John Stern*, and a Woman along with them, went round from Town to Town, through many Parts of *Essex*, *Suffolk*, *Norfolk*, and *Huntingtonshire*, to discover Witches. Several Clergymen preached, and spake against them, as far as those Times would suffer, and particularly Mr. *Gaul*, of *Stoughton* in *Huntingtonshire*, opposed very heartily that Trade that these People drove." In Suffolk a most sensational discovery was made when it was found that John Lowes, an old man above eighty years of age, who had for half a century been Vicar of Brandeston, was a witch. Although he had been minister in the same place for fifty years, it is to be noticed that he was continually quarrelling with his neighbours and had the common reputation of being an exceedingly litigious and unpacific individual. Baxter certainly says that he was a " reading " parson, which was the name given by the Puritans to those rectors and vicars who, according to the directions of the Book of Common Prayer, read Mattins and Evensong daily in their churches and did not exalt the sermon to a Sacrament, although as a matter of fact this seems a mistake; and, as Bishop Hutchinson says with reference to this passage, Mr. Baxter " knew who he wrote for, and that that would make them believe any Thing that was ill of him, upon a very slender Proof." In fact the very reverse was the case, for as a young man John Lowes had been summoned to appear before the Bishop's court at Ipswich on a charge of obstinately refusing to conform to the rites and ritual of the Established Church. In 1625 he had been indicted in the Ipswich courts, and yet again, not many years later, he was convicted by law as a " common imbarritor"; that is to say, one who for his own profit vexatiously foments and maliciously incites to litigation. What proved far more serious, however, was the fact that Lowes had already been once arraigned for witchcraft, and we can quite understand that when Hopkins got hold of him he had small chance of escape. The story which was wrung from him concerning his command to his familiar to sink a ship is characterized as " a monstrous Tale, without any tolerable Proof to support it," by Hutchinson, who in the course of investigating the present case wrote to Mr. Wilson, the then Vicar of Brandeston, and this gentleman put him in communication with a Mr. Rivett, who had long lived in the village and whose father before him had always resided there. Mr. Rivett replied to these inquiries in the following letter : " Sir, In Answer to your Request concerning Mr. *Lowes*, my Father was always of the Opinion, that Mr. *Lowes* suffered wrongfully, and hath often said that he did believe he was no more a Wizzard than he was. I have heard it from them that watched with him, that they kept him awake several Nights together, and run him backwards and forwards about the Room, until he was out of Breath : Then they rested him a little, and then ran him again : And thus they did for several Days and Nights together, till he was weary of his Life, and was scarce sensible of what he said or did. They swam him at *Framlingham*, but that was no true Rule to try him by ; for they put in honest People at the same Time, and they swam as well as he." We here find that at least three of Matthew Hopkins' favourite methods of detecting witches won scant credence even in his own day, and their utility was being pretty severely criticized. Hopkins, indeed, is at some pains to defend them in his own pamphlet, where he rather laboriously vindicates his accustomed practice in these matters.

The process of watching is thus described by John Gaule in his *Select Cases of Conscience Touching Witches* : "Having taken the suspected Witch, shee is placed in the middle of a room upon a stool or table, crosse-legg'd, or in some other uneasie posture, to which if she submits not she is then bound with cords ; there is she watcht and kept without meat or sleep for the space of 24 hours. . . . A little hole is likewise made in the door for the Impe to come in at ; and lest it might come in some less discernible shape, they that watch are taught to be ever and anon sweeping

THE
Diſcovery of VVitches:

IN

Anſwer to ſeverall Q u e r i e s,

L A T E L Y

Delivered to the Judges of Aſſize for the
County of N o r f o l k.

And now publiſhed

By M a t t h e vv H o p k i n s, Witch-finder.

F O R

The Benefit of the whole K i n g d o m e.

E x o d. 22. 18.

Thou ſhalt not ſuffer a witch to live.

---

may. 16

L O N D O N,

Printed for R. *Royſton*, at the Angell in Ivie Lane.
M. DC. XLVII.

The Witch Swims!

the room, and if they see any spiders or flyes to kill them. And if they cannot kill them when they may be seen they are her Impes." This seems to have impressed the general imagination, and there are various literary allusions to the watching, as in Shadwell's *A True Widow*, produced at Dorset Garden in December, 1678 ; 4to, 1679 ; V, where Theodosia says to Carlos : " I see you are resolved to watch me, to make me confess Love, as they do Witches, to make 'em own their Contracts with the Devil." In Mrs. Behn's *The Dutch Lover*, produced at Dorset Garden in February, 1672-3, I, 2, Marcel exclaims :

"There is a Knack in Love, a critical Minute :
And Women must be watcht as Witches are,
E'er they confess, and then they yield apace."

In *The City-Heiress*, one of Mrs. Behn's best comedies, produced at Dorset Garden in 1682, I, 1, Sir Anthony whispers to his nephew :

"Believe me, *Charles*, Women love Importunity.
Watch her close, watch her like a witch, Boy,
Till she confess the Devil in her,—Love."

The hurrying the accused to and fro and the running one forwards and backwards about a room is obviously nothing else than a form of torture. A similar torment was officially employed in certain districts of Germany, when to extort confessions wretched criminals were kept without sleep, and this may be paralleled in other lands.

The water-ordeal was considered supremely efficacious. The witches tied with " their thumbes and great toes . . . acrosse " and steadied by ropes—(" a roape tyed about their middles ")—were let down into the water, it might be a running stream or a still pond. If a witch swam her guilt was evident, for as she had rejected the sacramental laver of Baptism so now the water refused to receive her into its bosom. King James strongly advocates this test in his *Daemonologie*, saying: "It appeares that God hath appoynted (for a supernaturall signe of the monstrous impietie of the Witches) that the water shall refuse to receive them in her bosom, that haue shaken off them the sacred Water of Baptisme, and wilfullie refused the benefite thereof." It is remarkable that the belief in swimming a witch persisted late into the nineteenth century. Writing in 1861 Mrs. Lynn Linton speaks of an " old gentleman who died at Polstead not so long ago, and who, when a boy, had seen a witch swum in Polstead Ponds, ' and she went over the water like a cork ! ' " In 1865 at Castle Headingham two persons, a man and a woman, were charged with having assaulted an old Frenchman, whom they suspected of sorcery, by throwing him into a brook, whilst a rabble urged them on, yelling, " Swim him, swim him on the Millhead." The old man died within twenty-four hours of exposure and shock, and the prisoners were committed to the Chelmsford assizes. The bench commented on the " deep belief in witchcraft which possesses to a lamentable extent the tradespeople and lower orders of the district."

As early as the laws of Hammurabi, King of Babylon, in the third millennium B.C., water was appointed as a test in cases of sorcery. " If a man charges another with black magic and has not made his case good, the one who is thus taxed shall go to the river and plunge into the water. If the river overcometh him then shall his accuser possess his property. If, however, the river prove him innocent and he be not drowned his accuser shall surely be put to death, and the dead man's property shall become the portion of him who underwent the ordeal." The fundamental idea of the immaculate purity of water, which here destroys—or, as was more generally believed rejects—all that is unholy, is found throughout the world. This element has almost a divine character. It is present in the Holy Sacrifice of the Mass; it is an integral of the great Sacrament of Baptism; Holy Water availeth to cleanse from venial sin, it is often proved to have curative properties, it fills the heart with heavenly longings, and drives away the devil and his hosts, be they of earth or of hell. Sunday after Sunday the priest asperges his people with lustral purification. We cannot be surprised that at all times and in all places mankind has extolled the exceeding great virtue of fair water. The poet speaks of " waters at their priest-like task," and during the Eleusinian mysteries the initiate plunged into the sea to attain ritual purity, for as Euripides tells us: Θάλασσα κλύζει πάντα τἀνθρώπων κακά. (*Iphigeneia in Tauris*, 1193.)

In his *Religion of the Semites* (1889), Robertson Smith says: " Of all inanimate things that which has the best marked supernatural association among the Semites is flowing, or as the Hebrews say, ' living water.' . . . Sacred wells are amongst the oldest and most ineradicable objects of reverence among all the Semites." A little later (p. 163) mention is actually made of the practice of " swimming the witch." " In Hadramaut, according to Macrizi, when a man was injured by enchantment, he brought all the witches suspect to the sea or to a deep pool, tied stones to their backs and threw them into the water. She who did not sink was the guilty person, the meaning evidently being that the sacred element rejects the criminal. That an impure person dare not approach sacred waters is a general principle —whether the impurity is moral or physical is not a distinction made by ancient religion."

In England the swimming of a witch was actually the Judgement of God, the water ordeal, that might be applied for many crimes. It goes back to early days, about the sixth or seventh century, and a full description is given in the laws of Aethelstan, 924-940. After a preparation of prayer and fasting the person who was to undergo the test presented himself, and was bound the right thumb to the right great toe, the left thumb to the left great toe, and thus cast upon the water to sink or swim whilst Heaven's aid was invoked to decide the justice of the cause. If he sank he was innocent; if he swam he must be accounted guilty. Later there was introduced a change in the method of tying the accused; the right thumb was to be linked to the left big toe, the left thumb to the right big toe, so that the limbs would form the sign of the Holy Cross. This was the fashion employed in England during the seventeenth century and later, but the reason for this form had been obscured or completely forgotten. The code of S. Edward the Confessor prescribes the ordeal of water, and an oath with twelve compurgators was required. In certain cases thirty-six must be found, "et si alias de latrociniis composuerit est ad iudicium aquae."

Authorities, however, were very divided about the propriety and the efficacy of the ordeal, even if it were conducted, as was often the case in Elizabethan days, with much solemnity and parade under the supervision of the minister of the parish and his churchwardens. The people had no such scruple, and there was no livelier sport than to see a witch ducked. So general and deep-rooted was the common belief in this test that we even find suspects demanding to be subjected to it. Widow Coman, an Essex witch, who died in 1699, was at her own request thus experimented upon no less than three times. Hutchinson has a very significant passage (*Historical Essay Concerning Witchcraft*, Second Edition, 1720, pp. 175-6): " And as great Numbers of poor Creatures have been destroyed, and the Justice of the Nation reproach'd for this Custom of Swimming, and yet our Country-People are still as fond of it, as they are of Baiting a Bear or Bull : I will take leave to publish it in as solemn a Manner as I can; that at the Summer-Assizes held at *Brentwood* in *Essex*, in the year 1712, our Excellent Lord Chief Justice of *England*, the Right Honourable the Lord *Parker*, by a just and righteous Piece of Judgment, hath given all Men Warning, That if any dare for the future to make use of that Experiment, and the Party lose her Life by it, all they that are the Cause of it are guilty of *Wilful Murther*. . . . if any Man hereafter uses that ungodly Tryal, and the Party tried be drown'd; neither King *James'* Book, nor any other past Precedents will save them from an Halter." In 1751 a chimney-sweep, named Colley, was hanged for having headed at Tring, Hertfordshire, a disorderly rabble who ducked an old beggar, Osborne, and his wife, so that these poor wretches expired from ill-usage and exposure.

The Devil's Mark must be distinguished from the nipple by which the witch used to nourish her familiar. The *Lawes against Witches and Coniuration*, 1645, authoritatively stated that " their said Familiar hath some big or little Teat upon their body, wher he sucketh them : and besides their sucking, the Devil leaveth other markes upon their bodies, sometimes like a Blew-spot, or Red-spot like a flea-biting." Guazzo, in his *Compendium Malificarum*, tells us that this mark was a part of the admission ceremonies : " The Demon imprints upon the Witches some mark." This is mentioned by all demonologists. The spot was said to be invincible to pain, and when pricked, however deeply, it did not emit blood. Many cases, but by no means all, may of course be covered by the theory of callous malformations, thickened tissue, or birth marks, although it should be noted that with regard to the latter high authorities are very sceptical as to the effects of maternal impression upon the unborn child, and in this connexion the masterly study of Dr. Havelock Ellis, " The Psychic State in Pregnancy," *Erotic Symbolism*, must be read. It is noteworthy that the phenomenon of the " little Teat or Pap " so often found on the body of the witch seems to occur only in the records of England and New England. Of this there are very many instances, and here again a large number of cases may be explained by polymastia and polythelia, anatomical divagations which are far commoner than is generally supposed, and which have frequently been observed and described in recent medical treatises. But this

40

circumstance entirely fails to account for the details we find in such trials as those of the Burton witches in 1597 ; of Elizabeth Sawyer in 1621 ; of John Palmer, the S. Albans warlock, in 1649 ; of the Kidderminster witches in 1660 ; and many more beside.

Before Hopkins had been busy very long, from one hundred and thirty to two hundred people were imprisoned in the common gaol at Bury St. Edmunds upon multiplied accusations of witchcraft. In spite of the troublous times and the pressure of a political crisis the crusade had grown into such proportion that Parliament was bound to take notice of the proceedings, and "thereupon a special Commission of Oyer and Terminer was granted for the trial of these Witches." Serjeant John Godbolt presided over this court, which was composed of several Justices of the Peace together with two important ministers of Suffolk, Samuel Fairclough and Edmund Calamy. At the end of August the proceedings were opened by two sermons delivered by Mr. Fairclough at S. James's, Bury St. Edmunds. Eighteen persons, including two men, one of whom was John Lowes, were sentenced to be hanged, and " dyed . . . very desperately." But the special court was determined to put an end once and for all to the test of swimming, and this ordeal they prohibited in the most uncompromising terms, a measure which must have been something of a blow to Hopkins, who was notorious as a great favourer of the water experiment. There were still well-nigh one hundred and fifty persons in prison, and after a delay of three weeks or a month, during which interval the court broke up in some haste owing to the approach of the royal forces, a second session was held. Of the proceedings there is no exact record, but it seems probable that some forty or fifty witches were then condemned and doubtless hanged in due course, which means a pretty speedy execution. With regard to the rest their fate is unknown.

Before July 26th, owing to the activities of Hopkins, at least twenty witches were executed in the county of Norfolk, and on account of their great admiration of his energies the Corporation of Yarmouth, on August 15th, decided to summon him to their assistance, voting him full fees for his work. Yarmouth he visited twice, once in September and once in December. Six women were condemned, but of these one was respited. Later three women and one man were charged, but it does not appear that they were convicted. From Yarmouth he hurried to Ipswich, and it was here that Mother Lakeland suffered on September 9th. Although no doubt he was prominent in securing her conviction, he could not actually have been present at the execution, since we know that on September 8th he was much occupied in collecting evidence at Aldeburgh, a town he again visited on December 20th and January 7th.

At Stowmarket he must have made an exceptional haul, since he was paid no less than £23, a very considerable sum for those days. He also had the satisfaction of hanging two witches, Dorothy Lee and Grace Wright, at King's Lynn. Whilst he himself hurried from town to town it seems probable that the smaller villages were visited by his subordinates acting under his directions.

During the first months of 1646 he arrived in Cambridgeshire. Here the witches are said to have taken elaborate precautions to defend themselves from their enemy, and it appears that there were comparatively few executions, although this was probably the occasion referred to in Glanvill's *Saducismus Triumphatus*, part 2, Relation viii, where there is mention of the "examining certain Witches at *Castle Hill* in *Cambridge*," when the most notorious was hanged.[1] From Cambridge he tilted at full speed into Northamptonshire, and here he came across some very remarkable evidence. His next excursion led him into Huntingdonshire, a county famous in the annals of English sorcery for the exploits of the witches of Warboys in 1593. The local Justices of the Peace warmly seconded the efforts of Hopkins, but it was now that he met with a check, which seems to have been the turning point in his career. Mr. John Gaule, the Vicar of Great Staughton, preached a stirring sermon against the witch-finder, and this had so extraordinary an effect that although Hopkins had been invited to visit the town he hesitated and in the end contented himself with writing the following letter to one of Mr. Gaule's parishioners: "My service to your Worship presented, I have this day received a Letter &c.—to come to a Towne called *Great Staughton* to search for evil disposed persons called Witches (though I heare your Minister is farre against us through ignorance) I intend to come (God willing) the sooner to heare his singular Judgment on the behalfe of such parties; I have known a Minister in *Suffolke* preach as much against their discovery in a Pulpit, and forc'd to recant it (by the Committee) in the same place. I much marvaile such evill Members should daily preach Terrour

[1] London, 1681, pp. 208-9.

43

to convince such Offenders, stand up to take their parts against such as are Complainants for the King, and sufferers themselves with their Families and Estates. I intend to give your Towne a Visite suddenly. I am to come to *Kimbolton* this weeke, and it shall bee tenne to one but I will come to your Town first, but I would certainely know afore whether your Town affords many sticklers for such Cattell, or willing to give and afford us good welcome and entertainment, as other where I have beene, else I shall wave your Shire (not as yet beginning in any part of it myself) And betake me to such places where I doe and may persist without controle, but with thankes and recompence."

But Mr. Gaule was not a man to be frightened, and in 1646 he published his *Select Cases of Conscience Touching Witches and Witchcraft*, where he argues that the greatest caution must be used in admitting evidence. He has very serious doubts even when the accused confesses whether there may not be some delusion. He does not indeed deny that witches exist, but he does say that it is a matter of extraordinary difficulty to pronounce any person to be a witch however unequivocal the witness and the appearance of guilt.

None the less Hopkins was very busy during the March and April in Huntingdonshire. Exact details are missing, but it is certain that many were accused and several executed. In company with John Stearne he then passed into Bedfordshire, and it appears on record that they discovered witches in at least two villages. Elizabeth Gurrey of Risden made a full confession, and another woman declared that " at *Tilbrooke* bushes in *Bedfordsheir* . . . there met above

44

twenty at one time." There was, however, a growing opposition to Hopkins and all his works, and it is probable that after May, 1646, his activities entirely surceased, although it may be just possible that he was associated with Stearne in the discovery of witches in the Isle of Ely, when five persons were hanged. Although Hopkins, as Stearne tells us, died "peacibly, after a long sicknesse of a Consumption," at his old home in Manningtree, and although we have the actual entry in the parish register of Mistley-cum-Manningtree, "Matthew Hopkins, son of Mr. James Hopkins, Minister of Wenham, was buried at Mistley, August 12, 1647," yet poetical justice would have it otherwise, and the famous witch-finder who had earned for himself such hate and execration throughout the eastern counties of England was not to be allowed to go down to his grave in peace as a just and good man. Gossip and tradition were immediately busy with his memory. Even in his lifetime he had found it necessary to defend himself against the charge of being a wizard who had betrayed his fellows, and now this story was bruited in yet more elaborate detail. One story said that he had actually at some Sabbat filched the devil's private roll of all the witches in England. It was also reported that he had been swum in a pool and floated buoyantly over the surface of the water. Even so careful an inquirer as Bishop Hutchinson reports "that *Hopkins* went on searching and swimming the poor Creatures, until some Gentleman, out of Indignation at the Barbarity, took him, and tied his own Thumbs and Toes, as he used to tye others, and when he was put into the Water, he himself swam as they did. That clear'd the County of him ; and it was a great deal of Pity that they did nót think of the Experiment sooner."

This story is supposed to be supported by Butler's famous lines in *Hudibras*, Part H, Canto iii :

> "Has not this present *Parliament*
> A Legar to the *Devil* sent,
> Fully empower'd to treat about
> Finding revolted *Witches* out :
> And has not he, within a year,
> Hang'd threescore of them in one *Shire* ?
> Some only for not being *drown'd*,
> And some for sitting above ground,
> Whole *days* and *nights* upon their breeches,
> And feeling pain, were hang'd for *Witches*.
> And some for putting *Knavish* tricks
> Upon *Green-Geese* and *Turkey Chicks*,
> Or *Pigs*, that suddenly deceast,
> Of griefs unnat'ral, as he guest ;
> Who after prov'd himself a *Witch*,
> And made a Rod for his own *breech*."

Upon this there is a note : " The Witchfinder in *Suffolk*, who in the Presbyterian times had a commission to discover Witches, of whom (right or wrong) he caus'd sixty to be hang'd within the compass of one year, and among the rest an old Minister, who had been a painful Preacher for many years."

Butler's allusion, however, does not convey anything more than that Hopkins fell from his high estate, and died in obscurity, leaving a name loathed and reprobated throughout East Anglia and indeed all England. It is cer-

46

tain that the story of poetic retribution—that the witch-finder was himself swum—is a mere figment.

It may, at first sight, seem curious that Matthew Hopkins should be so prominent and so detested a figure in the annals of witchcraft. There were others who had executed far more than he. The Dominicans, John Nider, James Sprenger, and Heinrich Kramer; Paul Grilland; Nicolas Remy, Henri Boguet, Pierre de Lancre, in France; the Prince-Bishop of Bamberg, Gottfried von Aschhausen; and many other judges had sent larger numbers of witches to the stake and the gallows. But these judges had acted upon the highest authority; they had been thoroughly competent to inquire into these dark businesses of sorcery; their tribunals were established upon the firmest and soundest basis. Hopkins was, so to speak, a mere quack; a mountebank. He had neither the training nor the knowledge to deal with the hideous anarchy of witchcraft; his motive was vilest lust for gains, and this swept both innocent and guilty alike into his net. He desired not the glory of God but the fullness of Mammon. He did not fight against the armies of the devil but shed blood to fat his purse. He was no true man but a charlatan and a deceiver, " a monster of impudence and iniquity," one who plunged into deep and dangerous waters from no sense of duty, but
from an itch for notoriety, a greed for pelf—it was
not so much his crusade as his insincerity which
made his name stink in men's nostrils, which
causes him to be written down even to-
day as the foulest of foul parasites,
an obscene bird of prey of the
tribe of Judas and of Cain.

The Discovery of Witches

by Matthew Hopkins

CERTAINE QUERIES ANSWERED, WHICH HAVE BEEN AND ARE
LIKELY TO BE OBJECTED AGAINST MATTHEW HOPKINS, IN
HIS WAY OF FINDING OUT WITCHES

Querie 1. That he must needs be the greatest Witch, Sorcerer, and Wizzard himselfe, else hee could not doe it.

Answer. If Satan's kingdome be divided against itselfe, how shall it stand?

Querie 2. If he never went so farre as is before mentioned, yet for certaine he met with the Devill, and cheated him of his Booke, wherein were written all the Witches' names in *England*, and if he looks on any Witch, he can tell by her countenance what she is; so by this, his helpe is from the Devill.

Answer. If he had been too hard for the devill and got his book, it had been to his great commendation, and no disgrace at all : and for judgement in *Phisiognomie* he hath no more than any man else whatsoever.

Querie 3. From whence then proceeded this his skill ? Was it from his profound learning, or from much reading of learned Authors concerning that subject ?

Answer. From neither of both, but from experience, which though it be meanly esteemed of, yet the surest and safest way to judge by.

Querie 4. I pray where was this experience gained ? And why gained by him and not by others ?

Answer. The Discoverer never travelled far for it, but in *March*, 1644, he had some seven or eight of that horrible sect of Witches living in the Towne where he lived, a Towne in *Essex*, called *Maningtree*, with divers other adjacent Witches of other towns, who every six weeks in the night (being always on the Friday night) had their meeting close by his house, and had their severall solemne sacrifices there offered to the Devill, one of which this discoverer heard speaking to her *Imps* one night, and bid them goe to another Witch, who was thereupon apprehended, and searched by women who had for many yeares knowne the Devill's marks, and found to have three teats about her, which honest women have not : so upon command from the *Justice* they were to keep her from sleep two or three nights, expecting in that time to see her *familiars*, which the fourth night she called in by their severall names, and told them what shapes, a quarter of an houre before they came in, there being ten of us in the roome; the first she called was,

1. *Holt*, who came in like a white kitling.

2. *Jarmara*, who came in like a fat Spaniel without any legs at all, she said she kept him fat, for she clapt her hand on her belly, and said he suckt good blood from her body.

3. *Vinegar Tom*, who was like a long-legg'd Greyhound, with an head like an Oxe, with a long taile and broad eyes, who when this discoverer spoke to, and bade him goe to the place provided for him and his Angels, immediately transformed himselfe into the shape of a child of foure yeeres old without a head, and gave halfe a dozen turnes about the house, and vanished at the doore.

4. *Sack and Sugar*, like a black Rabbet.

5. *Newes*, like a Polcat. All these vanished away in a little time. Immediately after this Witch confessed severall other Witches, from whom she had her *Imps*, and named to divers women where their marks were, the number of their *Marks*, and *Imps*, and *Imps* names, as *Elemanzer*, *Pyewacket, Peckin the Crown, Grizzel, Greedigut &c.* which no mortall could invent; and upon their searches the same Markes were found, the same number, and in the same place, and the like confessions from them of the same Imps, (though they knew not that we were told before) and so peached one another thereabouts that joyned together in the like damnable practise, that in our Hundred in *Essex*, 29 were condemned at once, 4 brought 25 miles to be hanged, where this Discoverer lives, for sending the Devill like a Beare to kill him in his garden, so by seeing diverse of the mens Papps, and trying wayes with hundreds of them, he gained this experience, and for ought he knowes

any man else may find them as well as he and his company, if they had the same skill and experience.

Querie 5. Many poore people are condemned for having a Pap, or Teat about them, whereas many People (especially antient People) are, and have been a long time, troubled with naturall wretts on severall parts of their bodies, and other naturall excressencies as Hemerodes, Piles, Child-bearing, &c. And these shall be judged only by one man alone, and a woman, and so accused or acquitted.

Answer. The parties so judging can justifie their skill to any, and shew good reasons why such markes are not meerly naturall, neither that they can happen by any such naturall cause as is before expressed, and for further answer for their private judgements alone, it is most false and untrue, for never was any man tryed by search of his body, but commonly a dozen of the ablest men in the parish or else where, were present, and most commonly as many ancient skilfull matrons and midwives present when the women are tryed, which marks not only he and his company attest to be very suspitious, but all beholders, the skilfulest of them, doe not approve of them, but likewise assent that such tokens cannot in their judgements proceed from any the above mentioned Causes.

Querie 6. It is a thing impossible for any man or woman to judge rightly on such marks, they are so neare to naturall excressencies, and they that finde them, durst not presently give Oath they were drawne by evill spirits, till they have used unlawfull courses of torture to make them say any thing for ease and quiet, as who would not do ? but I would know the reasons he speakes of, how, and whereby to discover the one from the other, and so be satisfied in that.

Answer. The reasons in breefe are three, which for the present he judgeth to differ from naturall marks ; which are :

1. He judgeth by the unusualnes of the place where he findeth the teats in or on their bodies, being farre distant from any usuall place, from whence such naturall markes proceed, as if a witch plead the markes found are Emerods, if I finde them on the bottome of the back-bone, shall I assent with him, knowing they are not neere that veine, and so others by child-bearing, when it may be they are in the contrary part ?

2. They are most commonly insensible, and feele neither pin, needle, aule, &c., thrust through them.

3. The often variations and mutations of these marks into severall formes, confirmes the matter, as if a Witch hear a month or two before that the *Witch-finder* (as they call him) is comming, they will, and have put out their Imps to others to suckle them, even to their owne young and tender children ; these upon search are found to have dry skinnes and filmes only, and be close to the flesh, keepe her 24 houres with a diligent eye, that none of her spirits come in any visible shape to suck her ; the women have seen the next day after her Teats extended out to their former filling length, full of corruption ready to burst, and leaving her alone then one quarter of an houre, and let the women go up againe, and shee will have them drawn by her Imps close again : *Probatum est.* Now for answer to their tortures in its due place.

Querie 7. How can it possibly be that the Devill being a spirit, and wants no nutriment or sustentation, should desire to suck any blood ? and indeed as he is a spirit he cannot draw any such excressences, having neither flesh nor bone, nor can be felt, &c.

Answer. He seekes not their bloud, as if he could not subsist without that nourishment, but he often repairs to them, and gets it, the more to aggravate the Witches damnation, and to put her in mind of her *Covenant* : and as he is a Spirit and Prince of the ayre, he appears to them in any shape whatsoever, which shape is occasioned by him through joyning of condensed thickned aire together, and many times doth assume shapes of many creatures ; but to create any thing he cannot do it, it is only proper to God : But in this case of drawing out of these Teats, he doth really enter into the body, reall, corporeall, substantiall creature, and forceth that Creature (he working in it) to his desired ends, and useth the organs of that body to speake withall to make his compact up with the Witches, be the creature Cat, Rat, Mouse, &c.

Querie 8. When these Paps are fully discovered, yet that will not serve sufficiently to convict them, but they must be tortured and kept from sleep two or three nights, to distract them, and make them say any thing ; which is a way to tame a wilde Colt, or Hawke, &c.

Answer. In the infancy of this discovery it was not only thought fitting, but enjoyned in *Essex*, and *Suffolke* by the Magistrates, with this intention only, because they being kept awake would be more the active to cal their Imps in open view the sooner to their helpe, which oftentimes have so happened; and never or seldome did any Witch ever complaine in the time of their keeping for want of rest, but after they had beat their heads together in the Goale; and after this use was not allowed of by the Judges and other Magistrates, it was never since used, which is a yeare and a halfe since, neither were any kept from sleep by any order or direction since; but peradventure their own stubborne wills did not let them sleep, though tendered and offered to them.

Querie 9. Beside that unreasonable watching, they were extraordinarily walked, till their feet were blistered, and so forced through that cruelty to confesse, &c.

Answer. It was in the same beginning of this discovery, and the meaning of walking of them at the highest extent of cruelty, was only they to walke about themselves the night they were watched, only to keepe them waking : and the reason was this, when they did lie or sit in a chaire, if they did offer to couch downe, then the watchers were only to desire them to sit up and walke about, for indeed when they be suffered so to couch, immediately comes their Familiars into the room and scareth the watchers, and heartneth on the Witch, though contrary to the true mean- ing of the same instructions, diverse have been by rusticall people, (they hearing them confess to be Witches) mis-used, spoiled, and abused, diverse whereof have suffered for the same, but could never be proved against this Discoverer to have a hand in it, or consent to it ; and hath likewise been un-used by him and others, ever since the time they were kept from sleep.

Querie 10. But there hath been an abominable, inhumane, and unmerciful tryall of these poore creatures, by tying them, and heaving them into the water; a tryall not allowable by Law or conscience, and I would faine know the reasons for that.

Answer. It is not denyed but many were so served as had Papps, and floated, others that had none were tryed with them and sunk, but marke the reasons.

For first the Divels policie is great, in perswading many to come of their owne accord to be tryed, perswading them their marks are so close they shall not be found out, so as diverse have come 10 or 12 Miles to be searched of their own accord, and hanged for their labour, (as one *Meggs*, a Baker did, who lived within 7 miles of *Norwich* and was hanged at Norwich Assizes for witchcraft), then when they find that the Devil tells them false they reflect on him, and he, (as 40 have confessed) adviseth them to be swome, and tels them they shall sinke and be cleared that way, then when they be tryed that way and floate, they see the Devill deceives them again, and have so laid open his treacheries.

2. It was never brought in against any of them at their tryals as any evidence.

3. King *James* in his *Demonology* saith, it is a certaine rule, for (saith he) Witches deny their baptisme when they Covenant with the Devill, water being the sole element thereof, and therefore saith he, when they be heaved into the water, the water refuseth to receive them into her bosom, (they being such Miscreants to deny their baptisme) and suffers them to float, as the Froath on the Sea, which the water will not receive, but casts it up and downe,

till it comes to the earthy element the shore, and there leaves it to consume.

4. Observe these generation of Witches, if they be at any time abused by being called Whore, Theefe, &c., by any where they live, they are the readiest to cry and wring their hands, and shed tears in abundance and run with full and right sorrowfull acclamations to some Justice of the Peace, and with many teares make their complaints: but now behold their stupidity; nature or the elements reflection from them, when they are accused for this horrible and damnable sin of Witchcraft, they never alter or change their countenances, nor let one Teare fall. This by the way swimming (by able Divines whom I reverence) is condemned for no way, and therefore of late hath, and for ever shall be left.

Querie 11. Oh! but if this torturing Witch-catcher can by all or any of these meanes, wring out a word or two of confession from any of these stupified, ignorant, unintelligible, poore silly creatures, (though none heare it but himselfe) he will adde and put her in feare to confesse, telling her else she shall be hanged; but if she doe, he will set her at liberty, and so put a word into her mouth, and make such a silly creature confesse she knowes not what.

Answer. He is of a better conscience, and for your better understanding of him, he doth thus uncase himselfe to all, and declares what confessions (though made by a Witch against her selfe) he allowes not of, and doth altogether account of no validity, or worthy of credence to be given to it, and ever did so account it, and ever likewise shall.

1. He utterly denyes that confession of a Witch to be of

any validity, when it is drawn from her by any torture or violence whatsoever; although after watching, walking or swimming, diverse have suffered, yet peradventure Magistrates with much care and diligence did solely and fully examine them after sleepe, and consideration sufficient.

2. He utterly denyes that confession of a Witch, which is drawn from her by flattery, viz. *if you will confesse you shall go home, you shall not go to the Goale, nor be hanged, &c.*

3. He utterly denyes that confession of a Witch, when she confesseth any improbability, impossibility, as *flying in the ayre, riding on a broom, &c.*

4. He utterly denyes a confession of a Witch, when it is interrogated to her, and words put into her mouth, to be of any force or effect: as to say to a silly (yet Witch wicked enough) *You have foure Imps have you not?* She answers affirmatively, Yes: *Did they not suck you?* Yes, saith she: *Are not their names so, and so?* Yes, saith shee: *Did not you send such an Impe to kill my child?* Yes, saith she, this being all her confession, after this manner, it is by him accompted nothing, and he earnestly doth desire that all Magistrates and Jurors would a little more than ever they did, examine witnesses, about the interrogated confessions.

Querie 12. If all these confessions be denyed, I wonder what he will make a confession, for sure it is, all these wayes have been used and took for good confessions, and many have suffered for them, and I know not what, he will then make a confession.

Answer. Yes, in brief he will declare what confession of a Witch is of validity and force in his judgement, to hang a Witch: when a Witch is first found with teats, then sequested from her house, which is onely to keep her old associates from her, and so by good counsell brought into a sad condition, by understanding of the horribleness of her sin, and the judgements threatned against her ; and knowing the Devill's malice and subtile circumventions, is brought to remorse and sorrow for complying with Satan so long, and disobeying God's sacred Commands, doth then desire to unfold her mind with much bitterness, and then without any of the before-mentioned hard usages or questions put to her, doth of her owne accord declare what was the occasion of the Devils appearing to her, whether ignorance, pride, anger, malice, &c., was predominant over her, she doth then declare what speech they had, what likeness he was in, what voice he had, what familiars he sent her, what number of spirits, what names they had, what shape they were in, what imployment she set them about to severall persons in severall places, (unknowne to the hearers), all which mischiefs being proved to be done, at the same time she confessed to the same parties for the same cause, and all effected, is testimony enough against her for all her denyall.

Querie 13. How can any possibly believe that the Devill and the Witch joyning together, should have such power, as the Witches confesse, to kill such and such a man, child, horse, cow, or the like ; if we beleeve they can doe what they will, then we derogate from God's power, who for certaine limits the Devill and the Witch ; and I cannot beleeve they have any power at all.

Answer. God suffers the Devill many times to doe much hurt, and the devill doth play many times the deluder and impostor with these Witches, in perswading them that they are the cause of such and such a murder wrought by him with their consents, when and indeed neither he nor they had any hand in it, as thus : We must needs argue, he is of a long standing, above 6000 yeers, then he must needs be the best Scholar in all knowledges of arts and tongues, and so have the best skill in *Physicke*, judgment in *Physiognomie*, and knowledge of what disease is reigning or predominant in this or that man's body, (and so for cattell too) by reason of his long experience. This subtile tempter knowing such a man lyable to some sudden disease, (as by experience I have found) as *Plurisie, Imposthume*, &c., he resorts to divers Witches ; if they know the man, and seek to make a difference between the Witches and the party, it may be by telling them he hath threatned to have them very shortly searched, and so hanged for Witches, then they all consult with *Satan* to save themselves, and *Satan* stands ready prepared, with a *What will you have me doe for you, my deare and nearest children, covenanted and compacted with me in my hellish league, and sealed with your blood, my delicate firebrand-darlings.*[1] Oh thou (say they) that at the first didst promise to save us thy servants from any of our deadly enemies discovery, and didst promise to avenge and slay all those, we pleased, that did offend us ; Murther that wretch suddenly who threatens the down-fall of your loyall subjects. He then promiseth to effect it. Next newes is heard the partie is dead, he comes to the witch, and gets a world of reverence, credence and respect for his power and activeness, when and indeed the disease kills the party, not the Witch, nor the Devill, (onely the Devill knew that such a disease was predominant) and

[1] The Divelles Speech to the Witches.

the witch aggravates her damnation by her familiarity and consent to the Devill, and so comes likewise in compass of the Lawes. This is Satan's usuall impostring and deluding, but not his constant course of proceeding, for he and the witch doe mischiefe too much. But I would that Magistrates and Jurats would a little examine witnesses when they heare witches confess such and such a murder, whether the party had not long time before, or at the time when the witch grew suspected, some disease or other predominant, which might cause that issue or effect of death.

Querie 14. All that the witch-finder doth, is to fleece the country of their money, and therefore rides and goes to townes to have imployment, and promiseth them faire promises, and it may be doth nothing for it and possesseth many men that they have so many wizzards and so many witches in their towne, and so hartens them on to entertaine him.

Answer. You doe him a great deale of wrong in every of these particulars. For, first,

1. He never went to any towne or place, but they rode, writ, or sent often for him, and were (for ought he knew) glad of him.

2. He is a man that doth disclaime that ever he detected a witch, or said, Thou art a witch ; only after her tryall by search, and their owne confessions, he as others may judge.

3. Lastly, judge how he fleeceth the Country, and inriches himselfe, by considering the vast summe he takes of every towne, he demands but 20.s. a town, and doth sometimes ride 20. miles for that, & hath no more for all his charges thither and back again (& it may be stayes a weeke

there) and finde there 3. or 4. witches, or if it be but one, cheap enough, and this is the great summe he takes to maintaine his Companie with 3. horses.

Judicet ullus

THE END